RIGHT FROM WRONG

TruthWorks

OLDER CHILDREN'S EDITION

Josh McDowell

MANAGING WRITER

Dave Bellis

WRITERS

Cindy Ann Pitts   Christine Hockin-Boyd   Bonnie Bruce
Mark Swadley

World Bridge Press
127 Ninth Avenue, North
Nashville, Tennessee 37234

Distributed to the trade by Broadman and Holman Publishers

ISBN 0-8054-9830-3

Dewey Decimal Classification Number J231

Subject Heading: God–Will/Children–Religious Life

All Scripture quotations are from the Holy Bible, New International Version,
copyright © 1973, 1978, 1984 by International Bible Society.

Printed in the United States
of America

World Bridge Press
127 Ninth Avenue, North
Nashville, Tennessee 37234

Contents

Knowing Right from Wrong

LEARNING TO MAKE RIGHT CHOICES

"Do what is right and good in the Lord's sight"
Deuteronomy 6:18.

Sometimes it is difficult to make right choices. People often make choices based on how they feel. Some people will say that situations or circumstances will change what is right or wrong. Choices made based on our feelings or the situations we face can be choices which do not please God.

God, who made the world and created each person, gave us rules to help us live in a way which pleases Him. God has already decided that there are certain things that are right for all people, for all times, for all places. The Bible gives us clear guidelines which help us know right from wrong.

Over the next eight weeks, you are going to learn a better way to make choices. The Steps of Truth for making right choices are based on God's ideas and not on what people think. Look over the four Steps of Truth and hand motions below.

THE STEPS OF TRUTH

| CONSIDER THE CHOICE | COMPARE IT TO GOD | COMMIT TO GOD'S WAY | COUNT ON GOD'S PROTECTION AND PROVISION |

This study will help you learn more about each step and how to use the Steps of Truth to make right choices now and for the rest of your life.

My Truth Works Group

During the next seven weeks we will discover together how to make choices that please God. God is pleased when we cooperate and work together to learn more about choosing His way. Fill in the spaces below about yourself. Share "you" with your group.

My favorite fun thing to do is

_____

My Truth Works discussion group leader's name is

To me, God is

I go to _____ school.

My hair color is

I want to be called

My favorite color is

My favorite candy is_____

Why Should We
Fear God?

The Bible says, "The fear of the Lord is the beginning of knowledge" *(Proverbs 1:7)*. When we say "we fear God," it does not mean we are afraid of God because He might do something awful to us. It means that we respect Him because He is so powerful and good to us.

Match the reasons we should fear or respect God to the correct verse.

1. He is God.

2. He is the giver of all things.

3. He is the judge of good and evil.

4. It is for our own good.

A. "Every good and perfect gift is from above, coming down from the Father" *(James 1:17)*.

B. "For God will bring every deed into judgment, including every hidden thing, whether it is good or evil" *(Ecclesiastes 12:14)*.

C. "I will give them singleness of heart and action, so that they will always fear me for their own good" *(Jeremiah 32:39)*.

D. "Be still, and know that I am God" *(Psalm 46:10)*.

List six people you respect.

1. _____   4. _____

2. _____   5. _____

3. _____   6. _____

Why do you respect these persons? _____

_____

_____

Honesty
God Is True

"Do not steal. Do not lie. Do not deceive one another.
Do not swear falsely . . . Do not defraud your neighbor or rob him"
Leviticus 19:11-13.

God has many commands in the Bible which teach us to be honest. In today's Bible verse printed above, God says do not lie, do not cheat, and do not steal. God is not trying to make us follow a lot of rules just because He wants to boss us or to keep us from having fun. Being honest is really best for us! God wants us to be honest because He is honest. When we compare our attitudes and actions to God, we should want to be honest like God.

When we choose to be honest, God will protect us from guilt, shame, and bad relationships. We will be happier when we are honest because God will allow us to have a clear conscience, a sense of accomplishment, a good reputation, and the trust of other people.

GOD SAYS DO NOT	GOD SAYS DO
negative	*positive*
1. lie	A. respect other people's things
2. cheat	B. tell the truth
3. steal	C. complete your own work

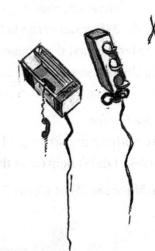

Truth Trials
Practicing the Steps of Truth

CASE ONE

I, Jeremy, the defendant, had two weeks to do a book report for school. I put off reading the book and played with my friends instead. The night before the book report was due, I realized there wasn't enough time to read the book and do the report. I remembered there was a movie about the book. If I rented the movie and watched it, I could make the report.

Consider the Choice
1. If I don't make the report, I will get a failing grade.
2. If I watch the movie and do the report from it, I might get an "A."

How Do I Make the Right Choice?

CASE TWO

I, Kelly, the defendant, and my friend were really thirsty and we only had enough money for one can of soda. I put the money in the soda machine. A can came out and our money came back in the coin return.

Consider the Choice
1. I could use the money to buy my friend a soda.
2. I could return the money to the people who owned the soda machine, and my friend and I would share one soda. We really wanted our own cans of soda.

How Do I Make the Right Choice?

CASE THREE

I, Carlos, the defendant, was staying home with my older sister. Our parents asked us to clean the house while they ran errands for three hours. After my parents left, I watched TV while my older sister cleaned the house. When my parents came home, they said: "Thank you both for making the house so beautiful. We are going to take you for ice cream for doing all this hard work." My older sister glared at me, but didn't say anything although she had done all the work.

Consider the Choice
1. If I say nothing my sister probably won't tell on me, and I'll get to go for ice cream.
2. If I confess I didn't help clean the house, my parents might not buy me ice cream.

How Do I Make the Right Choice?

Choosing God's Way

I Can Choose to Be Honest and True

Give an example of a time when you are tempted to lie, cheat, or steal. _____
_____

1. CONSIDER THE CHOICE—How can you decide what is right?
List the benefits and consequences of your choices.

If I choose _____
(to do what is wrong)

The benefits are	*The consequences are*
_____	_____
_____	_____
_____	_____

If I choose _____
(to do what is right)

The benefits are	*The consequences are*
_____	_____
_____	_____
_____	_____

2. COMPARE IT TO GOD—What does God say? "Do not steal. Do not lie. Do not deceive one another" *(Leviticus 19:11)*.

3. COMMIT TO GOD'S WAY—How can you choose to obey God in the situation about which you wrote?
_____
_____

4. COUNT ON GOD'S PROTECTION AND PROVISION—How can choosing God's way protect and provide for you?

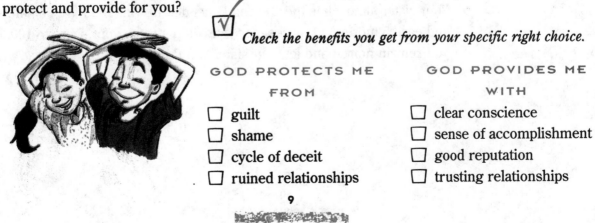

☑ *Check the benefits you get from your specific right choice.*

GOD PROTECTS ME FROM
- ☐ guilt
- ☐ shame
- ☐ cycle of deceit
- ☐ ruined relationships

GOD PROVIDES ME WITH
- ☐ clear conscience
- ☐ sense of accomplishment
- ☐ good reputation
- ☐ trusting relationships

Truth Detector

Use the Steps of Truth to find four honest attitudes and actions in this list. Mark the action *H* for Honest, *L* for Lying, *C* for Cheating, or *S* for Stealing.

_____ 1. Your parents sent you to the store with $10.00. The bill was $9.65. You kept the extra 35 cents because you felt you deserved the change for your effort.

_____ 2. You are riding your bike with your friends. You all start playing "wipe out" to see how close you can come to parked cars without hitting them. You go too fast and crash into the side of a car, leaving scratches and a dent. You tell the owner what you have done.

_____ 3. You ask your parents if you can go to the library for two hours. You go to the library for an hour and forty-five minutes and the video arcade for fifteen minutes. When your parents ask how the library trip was, you say: "Fine. I checked out two new books."

_____ 4. You go to use the pay phone at your school. When you deposit your quarter, several quarters come out the return slot. You take all the quarters and return them to the principal's office.

_____ 5. Your teacher has you exchange papers for grading. Your classmate overlooks the only wrong answer on your paper. You turn it in as a perfect grade.

_____ 6. You are playing a board game with your family and you are keeping score. Your sister almost has the 100 points needed to win. You have 94 points and earn 5 more. As scorekeeper you could stretch your score to 100, but you remain honest and let your sister win the game.

_____ 7. You go to the carnival on your 10th birthday. Ride tickets are $1.00 for ages two through nine and $2.00 for ages ten and up. You tell the ticket seller that you are nine to get the lower price.

_____ 8. Your team is one run behind in a baseball game. You hit a long ball over the left fielder's head. You run so fast around the bases trying to get home that you miss third base. The umpire doesn't notice and counts your run as good. You don't say anything, and let the run count.

_____ 9. Your teacher asks everyone to work quietly in their seats while she leaves the room for five minutes. You and two other classmates run around the room. When the teacher comes back, she says, "Those who did not stay in their seats, please raise your hands." You raise your hand and have to stay in at recess.

_____ 10. You are at your best friend's house and notice that he has a really neat set of colored markers. You tell him you wish you had some markers like that. He says: "Here, you may have them. I'll get some more from the art cabinet at school." You don't want to lose your best friend so you take the markers.

Purity
God Is Pure

"Do you not know that your body is a temple of the Holy Spirit, who is in you, whom you have received from God? You are not your own; you were bought at a price. Therefore honor God with your body"
1 Corinthians 6:19-20.

God is pure. God is perfect in every way. Because God is pure, He wants us to be pure. He cares for us more than our parents or anyone else could care about us. He knows that when we choose to follow His Way, we will be happier people.

God gave each person the gift of a body. Our bodies are special to Him. God's plan is that people respect their bodies and the bodies of others. God wants to protect us from harming our bodies with things that are not good for us, like illegal drugs or alcohol.

God gave us minds that can make many choices. God cares about the words we say because what we say comes from what we think. God wants us to have pure thoughts. What we see and read is important to God because if we see and read impure things, we will think about them.

God also wants us to keep our bodies pure because He wants us to worship Him. We need pure minds and bodies to truly worship Him. God says that our bodies are His temples because God the Holy Spirit lives in us.

WHAT DOES PURE MEAN?

- not mixed with anything else
- not containing anything dirty or hurtful
- clear
- not bad or evil
- virtuous
- just
- innocent

Which of the above words could be used to describe God? Pick four and write them below.

God is _____.   God is _____.

God is _____.   God is _____.

Because God is pure, He wants us to be pure, too!

My Body
God's Temple

"Do you not know that your body is a temple of the Holy Spirit,
who is in you, whom you have received from God? You are not your own;
you were bought at a price. Therefore honor God with your body"
1 Corinthians 6:19-20.

1. How is the body like a temple?

2. Why is it important to keep a temple clean?

3. Why should we want to be pure?

4. What does God want us to do with our bodies?

Choosing God's Way

Write in the space below a time you and your friends could be pressured to go along with the crowd and not keep your mind and body pure. _____

_____

1. CONSIDER THE CHOICE—How can you decide what is right?
   List the benefits and consequences of your choices.

   If I choose _____   If I choose _____
   (to do what is wrong)   *(to do what is right)*

   The benefits are   The consequences are   The benefits are   The consequences are

   _____   _____   _____   _____

   _____   _____   _____   _____

   _____   _____   _____   _____

2. COMPARE IT TO GOD—What does God say? "Keep yourself pure" *(1 Timothy 5:22b).*

3. COMMIT TO GOD'S WAY—How can you choose to obey God in the situation about which you wrote?

   _____

   _____

4. COUNT ON GOD'S PROTECTION AND PROVISION—How can choosing God's way protect and provide for you?

	GOD PROTECTS ME FROM	GOD PROVIDES ME WITH
	1. _____	1. _____
	2. _____	2. _____
	3. _____	3. _____
	4. _____	4. _____

Love
God Is Love

"Jesus replied: 'Love the Lord your God with all your heart and
with all your soul and with all your mind. This is the first and greatest commandment.
And the second is like it: Love your neighbor as yourself'"
Matthew 22:37-39.

The Bible teaches us that God is love. Love is something God feels. Love is something God does.
Most importantly, LOVE IS WHO GOD IS!

Look up and read *1 John 4:8-12, 16*, and *19*. Fill in the blanks below with the missing words
about God's love.

"Whoever does not love does not know God, because _____ ___ _____ . This is how
God showed his love among us: He _____ his one and only Son into the world that we might
_____ through him. This is love: not that we loved God, but that _____ _____ ____ and sent
his Son as an atoning sacrifice for our sins."

"Dear friends, since God so loved us, we also ought to _____ ____ _____. No one
has ever seen God; but if we _____ ____ _____, God lives in us and ____ _____ is
made complete in us . . . God _____ _____. Whoever lives in love lives in _____, and God in
him . . . We _____ because _____ _____ ____ ___ ."

THE MAIN POINTS

1. God is love.
2. God showed His love for us by
   sending Jesus to die on the cross
   as punishment for our sin.
3. God loved us first.
4. Because God loves us, we should love others.
5. When we love others, we show
   that God lives in us.

Read the verse printed under the session title. The verse says:

I should love _____ more than I love myself.

I should love _____ as much as I love myself.

 God's
3D Love Commands

LOVE COMMAND #1

"Love the Lord your God with all your heart and with all your soul and with all your mind"
Matthew 22:37.

I show love for God when I:

LOVE COMMAND #2

"Love your neighbor as yourself"
Matthew 22:39.

I show love for others when I:

LOVE COMMAND #3

"Love your enemies and pray for those who persecute you"
Matthew 5:44.

I show love for my enemies when I:

Choosing God's Way

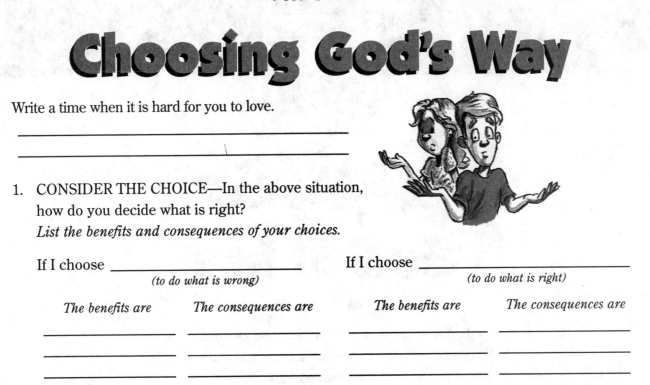

Write a time when it is hard for you to love.

_____

_____

1. CONSIDER THE CHOICE—In the above situation, how do you decide what is right?
List the benefits and consequences of your choices.

If I choose _____   If I choose _____
        (to do what is wrong)   *(to do what is right)*

The benefits are	The consequences are	The benefits are	The consequences are
_____	_____	_____	_____
_____	_____	_____	_____
_____	_____	_____	_____

2. COMPARE IT TO GOD—What does God say? "Love your enemies and pray for those who persecute you, that you may be sons of your Father in heaven" *(Matthew 5:44-45).*

3. COMMIT TO GOD'S WAY—How can you choose to obey God in the situation about which you wrote?

_____

_____

4. COUNT ON GOD'S PROTECTION AND PROVISION—How can choosing God's way protect and provide for you?

GOD PROTECTS ME FROM	GOD PROVIDES ME WITH
1. _____	1. _____
2. _____	2. _____
3. _____	3. _____
4. _____	4. _____

Justice
God Is Just

"He is the Rock, his works are perfect, and all his ways are just.
A faithful God who does no wrong, upright and just is he"
(Deuteronomy 32:4).

Everyone wants to be treated fairly. When someone does something wrong to you, you probably react by saying, "Hey, that isn't fair!" This shows that you feel it is right to be just and wrong to be unjust. Through the Bible God gave many commands to be just. The most important one is, "Do to others what you would have them do to you" *(Matthew 7:12)*. Doing to others as you want them to do to you is right because God is just.

Lead the children to read "The Pledge of Allegiance" and underline the last three words.

"I pledge allegiance to the flag of the United States of America and to the Republic for which it stands, one nation under God, indivisible, with liberty and justice for all."

This pledge states that in this country we want justice for all. What does that mean?

Why doesn't everyone always get treated fairly?

How does the verse above *(Deuteronomy 32:4)* describe God?

He is the_____.   He is _____.

His works are _____.   He does no_____.

All His ways are_____.   He is _____.

He is_____.

God is fair and He wants us to choose to be like Him.

Kid's Day in Court

Instructions of the judge to the jury

I order the jury to use the Steps of Truth to determine if the child in each case below was treated fairly.

CASE ONE

During recess Sara was selling candy bars for twenty-five cents for her class. Renee wanted to buy one. Renee had been mean to Sara and had thrown her notebook paper in the mud. So Sara sold Renee a candy bar for forty cents. Renee paid it because she did not realize it was only twenty-five cents. Sara kept the extra fifteen cents to help pay for the notebook paper Renee had ruined.

JURY

Was Sara right in what she did? _____

CASE TWO

Kyle and Bryce were playing a video game. They were only allowed to play for one hour. Kyle would not give up the controls because he was breaking his previous record. If he shared his video time with Bryce he would not make it to the next level.

JURY

Was Kyle right to want to keep playing?_____

Choosing God's Way

Justice and Me

Think about a time recently when you felt someone treated you unfairly. What did the person do? _____
_____

1. CONSIDER THE CHOICE—How can you decide what is right?
   A. What did you want to do to them? _____
      _____
   B. What was another choice you had? _____
      _____

2. COMPARE IT TO GOD—What does God say? "Do to others what you would have them do to you" *(Matthew 7:12)*.

3. COMMIT TO GOD'S WAY—Did you choose to obey God?
   A. In the situation above, were you just?_____.
      If you said yes, what makes you think you were just?
      _____
      _____
   B. If you said no, what makes you think you were unjust?
      _____
      _____

4. COUNT ON GOD'S PROTECTION AND PROVISION—How can choosing God's way protect and provide for you?

GOD PROTECTS ME FROM	GOD PROVIDES ME WITH
1. _____	1. _____
2. _____	2. _____
3. _____	3. _____
4. _____	4. _____

A Time to Get Even?

Joe has learned the Steps of Truth. How can he decide to say no to his selfish desire to get even with Bruce and choose to please God? Complete the comic strip showing how Joe can please God.

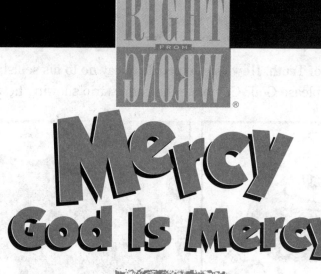

Mercy
God Is Mercy

"This is what the Lord Almighty says, 'Administer true justice:
show mercy and compassion to one another' "
(Zechariah 7:9).

We should be merciful because God is mercy. If you see a child who is hungry and you share your food, you are showing mercy. If you know someone who is sick and you send a card or pick flowers for him, you are showing mercy. If someone does something wrong to you and you forgive him, you are showing mercy. Sometimes, someone will do something wrong to you and will not even say he is sorry. If you forgive him anyway, you are showing mercy.

Why should we show mercy? We show mercy to others because God shows mercy to us. God chooses to show mercy to us even when we sin against Him. The Bible teaches us that everyone has sinned against God.

"For all have sinned and fall short of the glory of God" *(Romans 3:23).*

God showed us what true mercy was when He sent Jesus to die for our sin. When Jesus died on the cross, He was punished for our sin. When Jesus arose form the dead, He proved to us that He has the power to forgive us of sin. God shows His mercy by offering to forgive us of our sin. We can be thankful for the mercy God has offered to us through Jesus' death. We can pray and ask Jesus to take control of our lives and forgive us of our sin only because God is merciful.

COMPLETE THE BLANKS

All people have _____. *(See Romans 3:23.)*

God _____ Jesus to die and be punished for our sins. *(See John 3:16.)*

When we sin, we can ask G _____ to f _____ us. *(See 1 John 1:9.)*

God is m _____, so He will f _____ us.

God can help us choose H _____ w_____.

Choosing God's Way

Mercy Me! What Will I Do?

Your friend is sick. You want to buy a present for him. All your allowance is gone. You have been saving to buy a new video game. If you spend money for a present, you will not have enough to buy the video game. What will you do?

_____

1. CONSIDER THE CHOICE—How can you decide what is right?
   List the benefits and consequences of your choices.

   If I choose _____   If I choose _____
         (to do what is wrong)   *(to do what is right)*

   The benefits are   *The consequences are*   *The benefits are*   *The consequences are*

   _____   _____   _____   _____

   _____   _____   _____   _____

   _____   _____   _____   _____

2. COMPARE IT TO GOD—What does God say? "Show mercy and compassion to one another" *(Zechariah 7:9).*

3. COMMIT TO GOD'S WAY—How can you choose to obey God in the situation about which you wrote?

   _____

   _____

4. COUNT ON GOD'S PROTECTION AND PROVISION—How can choosing God's way protect and provide for you?

   ☑ *Check the correct answers*

   If you choose to show mercy, you can thank God for:

   ☐ making a friend happy   ☐ not helping a friend
   ☐ feeling good for   when he needed you
       doing what is right   ☐ feeling bad for not
   ☐ the appreciation your   doing the right thing
       friend expresses   ☐ blessings from Him

We Show Mercy

When We Forgive

In order to forgive someone, we must fully let go of the feelings caused by what the person did to us. To receive forgiveness, we must fully let go of our unforgiveness toward others.

Take a basketball in both hands, one hand on the left side and one hand on the right side. Both hands must fully hold the ball. Fingers must be flat against the ball. Ask someone to hold a dollar bill out to you. Try to take both ends of the dollar bill in one of your hands without your hands or fingers raising off the ball. You cannot use your wrists or arms to help hold the ball.

Why were you not able to take the dollar bill?

What would you have to do in order to take the dollar bill?

Use the words that go in the blanks to work the crossword puzzle and find how to be forgiven by God.

ACROSS

1. " _____ us our debts" *(Matthew 6:12)*.

2. "For if you _____ men" *(Matthew 6:14)*.

3. "But if you do not _____" *(Matthew 6:15)*.

4. "Your Father will not _____" *(Matthew 6:15)*.

DOWN

1. " _____, and you will be forgiven" *(Luke 6:37)*.

2. "If we confess our sins, he . . . will _____ our sins" *(1 John 1:9)*.

3. "Forgive . . . so that your Father in heaven may _____ you" *(Mark 11:25)*.

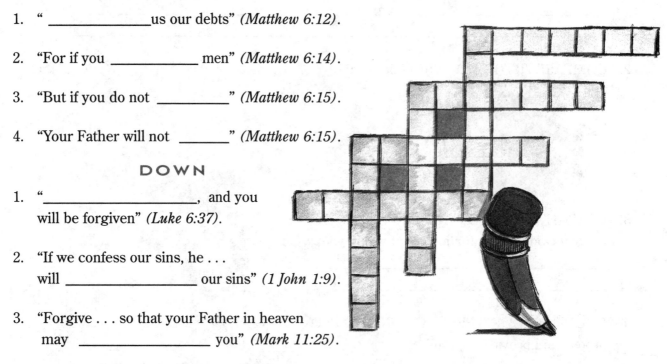

CIRCLE THE ANSWERS

1. To be forgiven by God we must forgive others: last   second   first

2. God says we must forgive others ten times the number of words in this puzzle plus seven.   70   77   47
   How many times must we be willing to forgive?
   When we forgive this many times, we are showing _____.

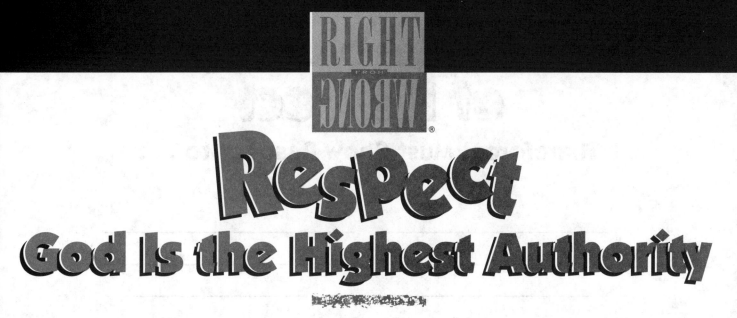

Respect
God Is the Highest Authority

"Show proper respect to everyone: Love the brotherhood of believers, fear God, honor the king"
1 Peter 2:17.

Who needs respect? You do! Everyone wants respect no matter their age, what school they attend, the style of clothes they wear, or the type of house in which they live.

We show respect to God because He is the highest authority and is worthy of respect. When you show respect to another person, you are showing respect to God. Look at a familiar Bible verse and discover for yourself a benefit for showing respect to your parents. Exodus 20:12 says, "Honor your father and your mother, so that you may live long in the land the Lord your God is giving you."

Wow! What's the benefit of showing respect to your parents? Underline the answer in the Bible verse.

The truth about respect is that we show respect to others and people in authority because God has placed them in authority over us. We show respect in order to obey God. We are also to show respect to people who do not have authority over us. We respect them because they are made in the image of God. Wanting to live a long life should not be the primary reason you show respect. We respect others because God is worthy of respect. God is a God of respect; therefore, I must respect others.

REVIEW TIME!
What is the reason we show respect? Make the right choice.

☐ The Bible tells me to show respect.   ☐ I can live a long life.   ☐ God is worthy of respect.

TRUE OR FALSE
_____ We show respect only to people who earn our respect.

_____ We do not have to respect little children who are younger than we are.

_____ God wants us to respect our parents.

_____ We do not have to respect a person who is not a Christian.

Everyone deserves respect. Read the Bible verse for today. Respect is to be shown to God, family members, friends, authority figures, and the law.

God Is Worthy of Respect

Therefore, I Must Show Respect to . . .

MY FAMILY

_____
_____
_____
_____
_____
_____

MY FRIENDS

_____
_____
_____
_____
_____
_____

AUTHORITY FIGURES

_____
_____
_____
_____
_____
_____

OTHERS

_____
_____
_____
_____
_____
_____

God is a God of respect; therefore, I must show respect to others.

I Was Disrespectful

Think of a time this past week when you were disrespectful to someone.
Describe what happened.

A FAMILY MEMBER

_____
_____
_____
_____

A FRIEND

_____
_____
_____
_____

AN AUTHORITY FIGURE

_____
_____
_____
_____

CHALLENGE FOR THE WEEK

Pray every day this week for God to help you show respect
to these individuals because God is a God of respect.

HOW DO I KNOW RESPECT IS GOOD FOR ME?

GOD PROTECTS ME FROM	GOD PROVIDES ME WITH
feeling put down	healthy self-esteem
harmful relationships	healthy relationships
not being liked	being liked by others
being talked bad about	praise

Choosing God's Way

Let's Make a Choice

Circle one of the following situations and go through the Steps of Truth.

    a.   to ridicule someone because of her looks

    b.   to becoming a gang member

    c.   to pick on someone who always does right

    d.   to constantly interrupt a teacher who is talking

1. CONSIDER THE CHOICE—How can you decide what is right?
List the benefits and consequences of your choices.

If I choose _____

The benefits are	The consequences are
_____	_____
_____	_____
_____	_____

2. COMPARE IT TO GOD—What does God say? "Show proper respect to everyone: Love the brotherhood of believers, fear God, honor the king" *(1 Peter 2:17).*

3. COMMIT TO GOD'S WAY—Based on what God says, I choose to do right. I SUBMIT to His way! I will _____
_____.

4. COUNT ON GOD'S PROTECTION AND PROVISION—How can choosing God's way protect and provide for you?

GOD PROTECTS ME FROM	GOD PROVIDES ME WITH
1. _____	1. _____
2. _____	2. _____
3. _____	3. _____
4. _____	4. _____

Self-Control
God Is in Control

"Be self-controlled and alert"
1 Peter 5:8a.

God wants us to be in control of ourselves. Controlling ourselves is something with which we deal every day. We can practice self-control in choosing the kinds of food we eat and the movies we watch. It takes self-control to do homework before playing outside with friends. We show our self-control in how we use money on clothes, videos, and music.

Showing self-control is the ability to withhold our selfish desires, actions, and attitudes. We need God's help to make the right choices. God wants us to allow the Holy Spirit's power to direct our self-control habits. It is important for us to demonstrate self-control because God is in control. Numbers 14:18 says, "The Lord is slow to anger, abounding in love and forgiving sin and rebellion." God uses self-control in showing His anger. When we look at the stars at night or see a sunrise, we are reminded that God is in control of the whole universe.

LET'S CHECK OUR KNOWLEDGE SO FAR

TRUE OR FALSE
Circle the right answers.

T F Self-control is easy!

T F God is sometimes in control.

T F God is slow to anger and responds to us with patience and love.

T F How I spend money does not matter to God.

T F When I do "my own thing," I am not practicing self-control.

DISCUSSION QUESTION
Have you ever thought of making a choice about self-control before you are in a situation that you have to make a choice?

Tough Times
for Self-Control

DECODE THE WORDS

Use the following code to discover ways that we need to practice self-control.

1 = a	4 = d	7 = g	10 = k	13 = n	16 = r	19 = u	22 = y
2 = b	5 = e	8 = h	11 = l	14 = o	17 = s	20 = v	23 = z
3 = c	6 = f	9 = i	12 = m	15 = p	18 = t	21 = w	

It is hard to practice self-control when we are ___ ___ ___ ___ ___ .
    1   13   7   16   22

When I lose my ___ ___ ___ ___ ___ ___ , I might be tempted to say
              18   5   12   15   5   16

___ ___ ___ ___ ___ ___ ___ ___ or ___ ___ ___ ___ others.
 2   1   4   21 14 16 4   17   8   19 16 18

God wants us to get rid of ___ ___ ___ ___ ___, ___ ___ ___ ___,
                            1   13   7   5   16   16   1   7   5

___ ___ ___ ___ ___ ___, ___ ___ ___ ___ ___ ___ ___ .
 12   1   11   9   3   5   17 11   1   13   4   5   16

(See Colossians 3:8.)

Some people are tempted to ___ ___ ___ ___ ___ ___ ___ or
                            14   20   5   16   5   1   18

___ ___ ___ ___ ___ ___ ___ ___ ___ ___ ___ unwisely. Others
 17   15   5   13   4   12   14   13   5   22

waste ___ ___ ___ ___ or use it in the wrong way, like watching too
      18   9   12   5

much ___ ___ ___ ___ ___ ___ ___ ___ ___ .
     18   5   11   5   20   9   17   9   14   13

Some people lose their self-control when they are with others. The Bible says we are not to get
___ ___ ___ ___ ___ with beer or alcohol. *(See Ephesians 5:18.)*
 4   16   19   13   10

God wants us to be in control of our minds and bodies.

Name a time when it is hard for you to practice self-control. _____

_____

Choosing God's Way
I Can Practice Self-Control

Think of a situation last week when you had a hard time practicing self-control.
What happened? _____
_____

1. CONSIDER THE CHOICE—What choices
   did you have in the above situation?

   I could _____

   The benefits are   *The consequences are*

   _____   _____
   _____   _____
   _____   _____

2. COMPARE IT TO GOD—What does God say? "Be self-controlled and alert" *(1 Peter 5:8a)*.

3. COMMIT TO GOD'S WAY—How can I submit to
   God's way? _____
   _____

4. COUNT ON GOD'S PROTECTION AND PROVISION—How can choosing God's way
   protect and provide for you?

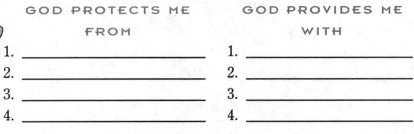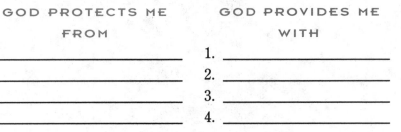

	GOD PROTECTS ME FROM		GOD PROVIDES ME WITH
	1. _____		1. _____
	2. _____		2. _____
	3. _____		3. _____
	4. _____		4. _____

Honesty
God Is True

Ask a parent or other adult to read with you the activities for each day. Answer the questions. Fill in the blanks with the words from this list (some words are used more than once): perfect, wrong, Father, true, work, truth, steal, laws, right. (Use the *New International Version* of the Bible.)

MONDAY
What it means to be honest
Memory Verse: Leviticus 19:11-13

Do not steal. Do not lie. Do not deceive one another. Do not swear falsely . . . Do not defraud your neighbor or rob him.
Do: When you have memorized the verse above, write it on the back of this page or say it from memory to an adult.
Pray: "Dear God, help me to be honest all the time."

TUESDAY
God is true.
We should be true
Read: John 14:6

Do: Jesus is God. What is Jesus like?
"Jesus answered, 'I am the way and the _____ and the _____ life. No one comes to the _____ except through me.'"
Pray: "Dear God, help me to be true like Jesus is true."

WEDNESDAY
God does not lie.
We should not lie
Read: Psalm 119:160

Do: Is God's Word true?
"All your words are _____; all your righteous _____ are eternal."
Pray: "Dear God, help me to tell the truth, even when it is difficult."

THURSDAY
God does not cheat.
We should not cheat
Read: Deuteronomy 32:4

Do: Is God fair?
"He is the Rock, his works are _____, and all his ways are just. A faithful God who does no _____, upright and just is he."
Pray: "Dear God, keep me from being tempted to cheat, and when I am tempted, help me do what is right."

FRIDAY
God does not steal.
We should not steal
Read: Ephesians 4:28a

Do: What does God's Word say to those who steal?
"He who has been stealing must _____ no longer, but must _____, doing something useful with his own hands."
Pray: "Dear God, help me not to steal. Help me do what is right."

Knowing
Right from Wrong

Ask a parent or other adult to read with you the activities for each day. Answer the questions. Unscramble the words to check your answers. (Use the *New International Version* Bible.)

MONDAY
Fearing God
Memory Verse: Deuteronomy 6:18

Do: Find the memory verse in your Bible and memorize it. When you have memorized it, write it below or say it from memory to an adult. _____
_____
Pray: "Dear God, help me to do what is right and good."

TUESDAY
Consider the choice
Read: Exodus 23:2

Do: What do you do when your friends want you to do something wrong? "Do not follow the c_____d *(orw)* in doing wrong."
Pray: "Dear God, help me not to follow my friends when they make bad choices."

WEDNESDAY
Compare it to God
Read: Job 34:12

Do: What is God like? Does He ever do anything wrong? "It is unthinkable that God would do w_____g *(orn)*."
Pray: "Dear God, I want to be like You. Help me make my choices based on what You are like."

THURSDAY
Commit to God's way
Read: Proverbs 3:5

Do: How do I choose to follow God's way? "T_____t *(usr)* in the Lord with all your heart and lean not on your own understanding."
Pray: "Dear God, help me to trust You and choose Your right way."

FRIDAY
Count on God's protection and provision
Read: Psalm 18:2

Do: Unscramble the words that describe God's protection/provision: "The Lord is my r_____k *(co)*, my fortress and my deliverer; my God is my rock, in whom I take refuge. He is my sh_____d *(lie)* and the horn of my salvation, my stronghold."
Pray: "Thank You, God, for protecting me and providing for me."

Challenge Activities

1. God is honest. We should be honest.
Read: Isaiah 45:19b
Do: When God speaks, what does He speak?
"I, the Lord, speak the _____; I declare what is _____."
Pray: "Dear God, let me speak true and honest words."

2. Write about when a friend was dishonest to you (he lied to you, cheated you, or stole from you). _____

How did his dishonesty make you feel? _____

What did it do to your friendship? _____

How can you show forgiveness to this friend? _____

God is also hurt when we are dishonest, but He will forgive us whenever we confess our sin to Him.

Read 1 John 1:9.
What is God faithful to do? _____

Live a life of truth and honesty. When you are dishonest, ask God to forgive you and keep trying to live honestly.

Challenge Activities

1. Read: Proverbs 1:7
The fear of the Lord is the beginning of knowledge.
When we talk about fearing God, what are we talking about? Choose the right answers from the list and write them in the space below:

forgetting Him   respecting Him
looking up to Him   listening to Him
honoring Him   being mean to Him
ignoring Him   obeying Him
wanting to please Him

2. Draw the four hand motions for the Steps of Truth.

1. CONSIDER THE CHOICE

2. COMPARE IT TO GOD

3. COMMIT TO GOD'S WAY

4. COUNT ON GOD'S CARE

3. Write about one of the choices you had to make this week where you used the Steps of Truth (use your journal). Talk to a parent or other adult about it.

Love

God Is Love

Ask a parent or other adult to read with you the activities for each day. (Use the *New International Version* of the Bible when looking up a Bible verse.)

MONDAY
Show God you love Him
Memory Verse: Matthew 22:37-39

Do: Take time to learn the verse and say it from memory to an adult.
Think of two ways you show God you love Him. Write them here and then do them.

1. _____
2. _____

Pray: "Dear God, help me to show You every day how much I love You."

TUESDAY
Show love to your family
Read: 1 John 4:7

Do: Make a list of the people who live with you.

_____
_____

How can you obey this verse today by loving the people with whom you live?

_____

Do the ideas that come to your mind.
Pray: "Dear God, help me to show my love to my family."

WEDNESDAY
Show love to others
Read: 1 John 3:11
This verse is almost the same as the one we read yesterday.

Do: Think of someone with whom you do not live for whom you can do something kind. Ask your parents to help you do something kind for him or her.
Pray: "Dear God, help me to show my love for

_____

this week."

THURSDAY
Love those who are mean to you
Read: Matthew 5:44

Do: This is a hard verse! Can you think of someone who is hard for you to love? Maybe a bully at school? Think of something nice you can do for him or her. Try to do it soon.
Pray: "Dear God, help me to love _____ She/he is hard to love, and I need your help to be able to love her/him."

Purity

God Is Pure

Ask a parent or other adult to read with you the activities for each day. (Use the *New International Version* of the Bible when looking up a Bible verse.)

MONDAY
Choose to honor God
Memory Verse: 1 Corinthians 6:19-20

Do you not know that your body is a temple of the Holy Spirit, who is in you, whom you have received from God? You are not your own; you were bought at a price. Therefore honor God with your body.

Do: Highlight or underline the last five words of this verse. Take time to learn the verse and say it from memory to an adult. How can you choose to honor God with your body today?

_____

Pray: Ask God to help you honor Him in everything you do today.

TUESDAY
Choose to please God when you watch TV
Read: Look at the words you marked yesterday in 1 Corinthians 6:20

Do: How many hours of TV do you watch in one day? _____ Before you watch TV today, pray and ask God to help you know when something is said or done on the show that does not please Him. Decide to quit watching the shows that are not good for you.
Pray: Ask God to help you watch only those TV shows that do not cause you to have impure thoughts.

WEDNESDAY
Choose to use words that please God
Read: 1 Timothy 5:22.

Do: Write the last three words of the verse here _____. Are there any words that you need to quit using? Decide to use words today that please God.
Pray: Ask God to help you use words that are pure.

THURSDAY
Choose to honor God with your body
Read: Review 1 Corinthians 6:20 (the last five words).

Do: Draw a picture of one thing you can do to take good care of your body. Put the picture in a place that will remind you to honor God today.
Pray: Ask God to help you honor Him by taking good care of your body.

God loved you first

Read: 1 John 4:19

Do: Circle the answer to the question: Who loved first, God or us?

Pray: Thank God for loving you. Sing a song to Him.

Challenge Activities

1. Do: Think of the most important thing you learned this week. Write it down below.

_____

_____

_____

_____

2. Think of one Bible story that talks about God loving us. Draw a picture from that Bible story.

3. Write about one of the choices you had to make this week where you had a chance to show love to someone (use your journal). Talk to a parent or other adult about it.

Choose to be pure like God is pure

Read: 1 John 3:3

Do: Find the Bible verse in your Bible and fill in the blanks below.

Everyone who has this _____ in him _____ him-self, just as he is _____.

Pray: Ask God to help you be pure like He is pure.

Challenge Activities

1. What does pure mean? Circle the words that describe what pure means.

dirty   good   clean   spotless   hurtful

bad   evil   clear   perfect

2. Write a prayer to God, thanking Him for the things you can do with your body that are pleasing to Him. _____

_____

_____

3. Write about one of the choices you had to make this week where you had a chance to be pure (use your journal). Talk to a parent or other adult about it.

_____

_____

_____

Mercy
God Is Mercy

Ask a parent or other adult to read with you the activities for each day.
(Use the *New International Version* of the Bible when looking up a Bible verse.)

MONDAY

God wants you to show compassion to others

This is what the Lord Almighty says, "Administer true justice . . . Show mercy and compassion to one another."

Memory Verse: Zechariah 7:9

Do: When you have memorized the verse above, turn the page and write it on the back of this page or say it from memory to an adult.

Pray: Ask God to help you grow up to be a person who shows compassion to others.

TUESDAY

Show compassion for the sick

Read: Matthew 25:36

Do: Think of someone who is sick. Make a card. Mail or take it to the person. Taking the time to make something shows you care. By doing this, you are showing mercy.

Pray: Ask God to help the person who is sick and the family. Pray also for the doctors who are taking care of the sick person.

WEDNESDAY

Show compassion for the poor

Read: Leviticus 19:10

Do: Give part of your allowance to help feed the hungry. Ask a parent or an adult to help you choose where to give your money.

Pray: Ask God to bless what you have given to feed the poor. Ask Him to multiply what you have given.

THURSDAY

Show compassion for someone who has treated you unkindly

Read: Mark 11:25

Do: Think of someone who has treated you unkindly. Tell God that you are willing to forgive the person. Then forget what he did to you. This is the way to show that you truly forgive.

Pray: Ask God to help you forgive that person. Ask God to help you treat that person as if he had never been unkind to you.

FRIDAY

Show compassion to those that are unhappy

Read: 1 Corinthians 16:18

Do: Think of someone who is unhappy. Draw a happy picture and take or mail it to that person. This is a way to show you care. When you care enough to do something, you are showing mercy.

Pray: Ask God to help you refresh the spirit of the person who is unhappy.

Justice
God Is Just

Ask a parent or other adult to read with you the activities for each day.
(Use the *New International Version* of the Bible when looking up a Bible verse.)

MONDAY

God is just so I should be just

He is the Rock, his works are perfect, and all his ways are just. A faithful God who does no wrong, upright and just is he.

Memory Verse: Deuteronomy 32:4

Do: When you have memorized the verse above, turn the page and write it on the back of this page or say it from memory to an adult.

Pray: "Dear God, help me to be just when I play and when I work."

TUESDAY

God takes care of those who are just

Read: 2 Thessalonians 1:6

Do: God is what? _____.
Think of someone you have treated unfairly. Use the Steps of Truth to decide how to treat her the next time.

Pray: "Dear God, help me to be fair with others even when they are not being fair with me."

WEDNESDAY

God wants to be good to us

Read: Isaiah 30:18

Do: What does God want to do? He wants to show us _____ .

Pray: "Dear God, thank You for showing us mercy and for being just."

THURSDAY

God loves justice

Read: Psalm 99:4

The King [God] is mighty, he loves justice—you have established equity . . . you have done what is just and right.

Do: Talk to a parent or other adult about why God would love justice (answer on the back of the page).

Pray: "Dear God, thank You for not having favorites. Help me to be the same way with the people around me."

KEY WORDS

Mighty....very powerful

Justice.....to do what is right and fair

Equity.....to treat others without having favorites

Challenge Activities

1. Read Luke 6:35. Think of one person whom you really have a hard time forgiving. Pray for that person every day for five days. Ask God to bless this person and to help you forgive him.

☑ *Check the box after you have prayed each time.*

☐ Day 1

☐ Day 2

☐ Day 3

☐ Day 4

☐ Day 5

2. Write about one of the choices you had to make this week where you had a chance to show mercy to someone (use your journal). Talk to a parent or other adult about it.

[Answer to Thursday's question: God loves justice because He wants for us to get along and live in peace. When we treat one another justly, we can live in peace and get along with each other better.]

FRIDAY

God wants you can do what the Bible says.
to follow justice

Do: Whose example should you follow? Name one way you can do what the Bible says.
Read: Deuteronomy 16:20
Pray: "Dear God, help me to do what is just and right even when no one but You is watching."

Challenge Activities

1. *Read:* Deuteronomy 32:4
Do: Admit that God is just. Admit that you should be just, too. God's ways are what?
Pray: "Dear God, help me to be just like You—not to have any favorites, to treat everyone right, and to love to do what is right all the time, everywhere."

2. Write about one of the choices you had to make this week where you had a chance to be fair and just to someone (use your journal). Talk to a parent or other adult about it.

Self-Control
God Is in Control

Ask a parent or other adult to read with you the activities for each day. (Use the New International Version of the Bible when looking up a Bible verse.)

MONDAY
God wants to help you have self-control
Memory Verse:
1 Peter 5:8

Be self-controlled and alert.
Do: When you have memorized the verse above, turn the page and write it on the back of this page or say it from memory to an adult.
Pray: Ask God to help you be alert to the things that might tempt you to lose control.

TUESDAY
God shows self-control
Read: Genesis 6:5-22; 7:1-8:17; 9:13-15

Do: Read this Bible story together with a parent. Discuss how God showed self-control. What was the beautiful promise that God gave us as a reminder each time we see it in the sky? _____ a i _____ b _____ w
Pray: Thank God for showing self-control in dealing with us.

WEDNESDAY
Show self-control when we speak
Read: Ephesians 5:4

Do: Write below the three things the verse says we should not do when we talk.
1. _____
2. _____
3. _____
Write the one thing the verse says we should do when we talk.
Pray: Ask God to help you show self-control when you talk to your parents, your teachers, your friends, and others.

THURSDAY
Show self-control when you feel angry
Read: Colossians 3:8

Do: Write below two things the verse mentions where you can show self-control.
1. _____
2. _____
Pray: Ask God to help you show self-control when you get angry.

Respect
God Is the Highest Authority

Ask a parent or other adult to read with you the activities for each day. (Use the *New International Version* of the Bible when looking up a Bible verse.)

MONDAY
God wants us to show respect to others
Memory Verse:
1 Peter 2:17

Show proper respect to everyone: Love the brotherhood of believers, fear God, honor the king.
Do: When you have memorized the verse above, turn the page and write it on the back of this page or say it from memory to an adult.
Pray: Thank God for the people around you to whom you are always happy to show respect.

TUESDAY
Show respect to God
Read: Exodus 3:4-6

Do: Whom did God ask to remove his sandals? _____
Was this showing respect to God? _____
Pray: Ask God for a good attitude when talking to Him.

WEDNESDAY
Show respect for leaders
Read: 1 Samuel 24:8-10

Do: What did David do to show respect for King Saul?
_____
Pray: Ask God to help you show respect for leaders.

THURSDAY
Show respect for those no one wants to respect
Read: 1 Samuel 30:11-15

Do: What group of people left a slave to die? _____
David and his men fed the slave a cake of pressed f___g___ and two cakes of ra___s___n___.
Pray: Tell God that you will treat with respect the people others do not want to respect.

FRIDAY
Show respect for your parents
Read: Exodus 20:12

Honor your father and your mother, so that you may live long in the land your God has given you.
Do: In the Bible verse above, circle the word that tells you what you are supposed to do. You honor your parents when you show respect for them and obey them. In the Bible verse above, underline the promise that God gives you if you obey the command.
Pray: Ask God to help you show respect to your parents every day and everywhere.

Prepare yourself to show self-control

Read: 1 Peter 1:13

Do: Talk to a parent or other adult about how we can be prepared to act right when an opportunity comes to show self-control.

Pray: Pray and ask God to help you be self-controlled in all your actions.

Challenge Activities

1. Write about one of the choices you had to make this week where you had a chance to show self-control (use your journal). Talk to a parent or other adult about it.

2. Write one time when it is very hard for you to show self-control. _____

Choose to pray every day for five days and ask God to help you show self-control with this one thing. Ask one of your parents or an adult to help you pray about this.

☑ *Check the box for every day you remember to pray.*

- ☐ Day 1
- ☐ Day 2
- ☐ Day 3
- ☐ Day 4
- ☐ Day 5

Challenge Activities

1. Draw a picture of one time this week when you saw someone showing respect. Talk to a parent or other adult about it

2. Write about one of the choices you had to make this week where you had a chance to show respect to someone (use your journal). Talk to a parent or other adult about it.